THE ULTIMATE
DALLAS COWBOYS
TRIVIA BOOK

A Collection of Amazing Trivia Quizzes
and Fun Facts for Die-Hard Cowboys Fans!

Ray Walker

ISBN: 978-1-953563-01-9

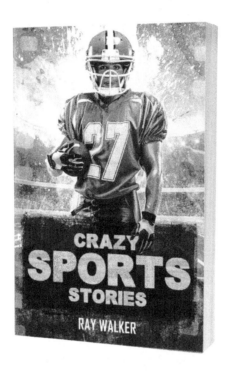

CONTENTS

INTRODUCTION

Team fandom should be inspirational. Our attachment to our favorite teams should fill us with pride, excitement, loyalty, and a sense of fulfillment in knowing that we are part of a community with many other fans who feel the same way.

Dallas Cowboys fans are no exception. With a long, rich tradition in the NFL, the Cowboys have inspired their supporters for sixty years with their history of colorful players, memorable eras, big moves, and unique moments.

This book is meant to be a celebration of those moments and an examination of the collection of interesting, impressive, or important details that allow us to understand the full stories behind the players and the team.

You may use the book as you wish. Each chapter contains twenty quiz questions in a mixture of multiple choice/true or false formats, an answer key (Don't worry, it's on a separate page!), and a section of ten "Did You Know" factoids about the team.

Some will use it to test themselves with the quiz questions. How much Cowboys history did you really know? How many of the finer points can you remember? Some will use it competitively (Isn't that the heart of sports?), waging contests with friends and fellow devotees to see who can lay claim to being the biggest fan. Some will enjoy it as a learning experience, gaining insight to enrich their fandom and add color to their understanding of their favorite team. Still others may use it to teach, sharing the wonderful anecdotes inside to inspire a new generation of fans to hop aboard the Dallas bandwagon.

Whatever your purpose may be, we hope you enjoy delving into the amazing background of America's Team...the Dallas Cowboys!

Oh...and for the record, information and statistics in this book are current up to the beginning of 2020. The Cowboys will surely topple more records and win more awards as the seasons pass, so keep this in mind when you're watching the next game with your friends, and someone starts a conversation with "Did you know...?".

CHAPTER 1:

ORIGINS & HISTORY

QUIZ TIME!

1. In which year was the Dallas Cowboys football team founded?

    a. 1940

    b. 1950

    c. 1955

    d. 1960

2. The Dallas football franchise has, at some point, been included in both the Western Conference and the Eastern Conference within the NFL's division of teams.

    a. True

    b. False

3. For the first decade of their existence, the Cowboys played all of their home games at which location?

    a. Texas Stadium

    b. Cotton Bowl

    c. Astrodome

    d. Dallas Municipal Field

4. The official Dallas Cowboys Team Headquarters is located in which Texas city?

    a. Dallas
    b. Arlington
    c. Frisco
    d. El Paso

5. Dallas has hosted a Thanksgiving Day game in each season since 1966, except for two years in which the NFL commissioner replaced them with another team. Which team took their spot during those two seasons, before bad ratings convinced the commissioner to change his mind?

    a. St. Louis Cardinals
    b. San Francisco 49ers
    c. Green Bay Packers
    d. New England Patriots

6. Why did many parties within the league's management originally think that an NFL football team would not be able to survive in Dallas?

    a. The players would not be able to last for full games in the intense Texas heat.
    b. There was not enough financial support from big, influential corporations in the area.
    c. The travel to and from Texas was too far for all the northern teams to manage it.
    d. Texans were too attached to high school and college football to care about the professional game.

7. The Dallas Cowboys won more games than any other NFL team during the period between 1970-1979.

    a. True

    b. False

8. How many seasons went by before the Cowboys recorded their first ever winning season?

    a. 0

    b. 2

    c. 5

    d. 7

9. The Cowboys are one of two NFL teams that host a Thursday Thanksgiving game annually; who is the other team?

    a. Green Bay Packers

    b. Detroit Lions

    c. Kansas City Chiefs

    d. New York Jets

10. In which year did billionaire oil magnate Jerry Jones take over as primary owner of the Cowboys?

    a. 1974

    b. 1982

    c. 1989

    d. 1998

11. What was the original name of the Dallas Cowboys cheerleading squad?

    a. Dallas Cowgirls

b. CowBelles & Beaux

c. America's Sweethearts

d. Dallas Cowboy Cheerleaders

12. In Dallas's first year in the NFL, they were not allowed to participate in the league's annual college entry draft.

a. True

b. False

13. AT&T Stadium, the current home of the Cowboys, is located in which city?

a. Dallas

b. Arlington

c. San Antonio

d. Austin

14. The shortest ownership term for a Dallas Cowboys owner is held by H.R. Bright. For how long did he own the team?

a. 48 days

b. 6 months

c. 1 year

d. 5 years

15. In which year did the Cowboys first add their mascot, Rowdy, in an attempt to improve the home game experience for fans?

a. 1970

b. 1983

c. 1996

d. 2008

16. According to a Forbes magazine evaluation, the Dallas Cowboys are financially the highest valued sports franchise in the world.

    a. True
    b. False

17. Which player scored the very first touchdown in Dallas Cowboys history?

    a. Roger Staubach
    b. Darryl Hannah Jr.
    c. Jim Doran
    d. Eddie LeBaron

18. The traditional Dallas Cowboys fight song, which was created by the Tom Merriman Big Band, is called what?

    a. "Call in the Cowboys"
    b. "Born to be a Cowboy"
    c. "Cowboys Stampede March"
    d. "Dallas on Patrol"

19. In 1967, the Cowboys faced the Green Bay Packers for the NFL Championship in a game dubbed the "Ice Bowl" due to frigid field conditions that reached NFL record lows. How cold was it?

    a. 6 degrees Fahrenheit
    b. 0 degrees Fahrenheit
    c. -4 degrees Fahrenheit
    d. -13 degrees Fahrenheit

20. When the NFL expanded south to Texas, Dallas was their second-choice city, after Houston, because Houston was considered a much larger television market.

    a. True
    b. False

QUIZ ANSWERS

1. D – 1960

2. A – True

3. B – Cotton Bowl

4. C – Frisco

5. A – St. Louis Cardinals

6. D – Texans were too attached to high school and college football to care about the professional game.

7. A – True

8. C – 5

9. B – Detroit Lions

10. C – 1989

11. B – CowBelles & Beaux

12. A – True

13. B – Arlington

14. D – 5 years

15. C – 1996

16. A – True

17. C – Jim Doran

18. C – "Cowboys Stampede March"

19. D – -13 degrees Fahrenheit

20. B – False

DID YOU KNOW?

1. For years, Cowboys founder Clint Murchison was blocked from adding a team in Dallas by one vote— Redskins owner George Marshall. Murchison sneakily purchased the rights to a song written by Marshall's wife, called "Hail to the Redskins." In exchange for allowing it to be played at Redskins games, Marshall switched his vote and the Cowboys were born.

2. The Dallas Cowboys cheerleading squad is perhaps the most famous in America. They have appeared on such hit TV shows as *The Love Boat*, *Family Feud*, *Saturday Night Live*, and *Hard Knocks*, and are often hired for events outside the Cowboys' games.

3. The Cowboys have played in three home locations. The Cotton Bowl was built decades before they became a franchise. Texas Stadium was built in 1971 for $35 million dollars. And, in 2009, AT&T Stadium was finished at a cost of $1.3 billion dollars. It was the biggest domed stadium anywhere on earth.

4. Before ever playing a game, the franchise was known by the league as the Dallas Steers. Their first general manager, Tex Schramm, changed it to the Dallas Rangers because he did not like how the fact that steers are castrated would reflect on his football team. The Rangers name conflicted with a minor league baseball team, so everyone settled on the Cowboys.

5. AT&T Stadium, for a time, was home to the country's largest scoreboard. It measures 160 feet long and 72 feet high. It is so large that punters have occasionally hit it with the football, creating chaos on the field below.

6. Dallas did not achieve much success on the field during their inaugural season. However, they did not lose every game. A tie with the New York Giants salvaged a 0-11-1 season.

7. During their first few years playing in the Cotton Bowl, the Cowboys shared the stadium with the AFL expansion team the Dallas Texans. The Texans would move and go on to become the Kansas City Chiefs, who eventually joined the NFL when the two leagues merged.

8. The Cowboys routinely set records for NFL attendance. They still hold the single game mark for most fans in the stadium, with 112,376. However, this record was not achieved in Dallas, but during an international game in Mexico City, in 1994.

9. Legendary Cowboy head coach Tom Landry coached winning football for so many seasons with the team that five of his assistants became head coaches with other franchises. Those coaches included Raymond Berry, Gene Stallings, Mike Ditka, John Mackovic, and Dan Reeves.

10. Dallas got it right with their first franchise hires. General manager Tex Schramm, coach Tom Landry, and director of player personnel Gil Brandt all remained in their positions with the team for an incredible 29 years.

CHAPTER 2:

JERSEYS & NUMBERS

QUIZ TIME!

1. How many stripes run from back to crown on the Cowboys helmet design?

   a. 0
   b. 1
   c. 2
   d. 3

2. The blue jerseys worn by Dallas are often said to have been "jinxed," and therefore the team avoids wearing them during the Super Bowl whenever the choice is theirs.

   a. True
   b. False

3. Two excellent Dallas wide receivers each wore number 88 for a decade with the team. Who were these two receivers?

   a. Billy Joe Dupree and Dez Bryant

    b. Alvin Harper and Terry Glenn

    c. Drew Pearson and Michael Irvin

    d. Tony Hill and Cole Beasley

4. In which year was the white outline (surrounded by a blue border) added to the iconic Dallas Cowboys star logo?

    a. 1961

    b. 1964

    c. 1980

    d. 1995

5. What year did the Cowboys start placing players' last names on the back of the jerseys?

    a. 1964

    b. 1970

    c. 1984

    d. 1986

6. Ten players have worn number 10 for the Cowboys. Which of these players scored the most career touchdowns?

    a. Ron Widby

    b. Reggie Collier

    c. Tavon Austin

    d. Jimmy Armstrong

7. Uniform number 3 is traditionally a kicker's number for the Cowboys, worn by Billy Cundiff, Eddie Murray, Richie Cunningham, and Kai Forbath. But it has also been sported by quarterbacks Jon Kitna and Steve Walsh.

a. True

b. False

8. Which of the following Cowboys players wore number 99 on his jersey?

   a. Leon Lett

   b. Chris Canty

   c. Hollywood Henderson

   d. Deion Sanders

9. Two Cowboys Hall-of-Famers wore number 22 during their time on the squad. Which two were they?

   a. Bob Hayes and Emmitt Smith

   b. Roger Staubach and Troy Aikman

   c. Bob Lilly and Drew Pearson

   d. Ed Jones and Charles Haley

10. The current version of the Cowboys uniform includes three colors. Which of the following is not included in the color scheme?

    a. Navy blue

    b. Royal blue

    c. Metallic silver

    d. Black

11. Hall of Fame defensive lineman Bob Lilly retired in the same year as the jersey number he wore. Which number was that?

    a. 70

    b. 72

c. 74

d. 76

12. The Cowboys have retired more jersey numbers than any other NFL franchise has.

    a. True
    b. False

13. Which two flashy but talented Cowboys both wore number 21 for the team?

    a. Deion Sanders and Ezekiel Elliott
    b. Hollywood Henderson and Michael Irvin
    c. Charles Haley and Emmitt Smith
    d. Don Meredith and Jaylon Smith

14. Which Cowboy wore lucky number 7 for the highest number of games played with the team?

    a. Bob Lilly
    b. DeMarco Murray
    c. Drew Henson
    d. Steve Beuerlein

15. The most popular number in Cowboys history has been worn by a total of 27 players. Which number saw this most widespread use?

    a. 99
    b. 55
    c. 9
    d. 23

16. No Cowboy has ever been brave enough to challenge superstition and wear unlucky number 13 on the back of his jersey.

    a. True
    b. False

17. Only one Cowboys player aside from Hall of Fame QB Troy Aikman has worn number 8 for the franchise. Who else did it?

    a. Buzz Sawyer
    b. Jason Witten
    c. Dan Bailey
    d. Leon Lett

18. Three big-name free agent wide receivers have come to Dallas and worn number 19. Which of the following chose a different number upon his arrival?

    a. Lance Alworth
    b. Amari Cooper
    c. Keyshawn Johnson
    d. Terrell Owens

19. Franchise icon Roger Staubach wore what number during his Cowboys career?

    a. 5
    b. 9
    c. 12
    d. 21

20. Cowboys running back Tony Dorsett wore four different numbers with the franchise, as he enjoyed "selling the rights" to numbers that other players wanted to wear.

   a. True
   b. False

QUIZ ANSWERS

1. D – 3

2. A – True

3. C – Drew Pearson and Michael Irvin

4. B – 1964

5. B – 1970

6. C – Tavon Austin

7. A – True

8. B – Chris Canty

9. A – Bob Hayes and Emmitt Smith

10. D – Black

11. C – 74

12. B – False

13. A – Deion Sanders and Ezekiel Elliott

14. D – Steve Beuerlein

15. D – 23

16. B – False

17. A – Buzz Sawyer

18. D – Terrell Owens

19. C – 12

20. B – False

DID YOU KNOW?

1. Each Cowboys helmet has a small strip of blue tape affixed on the white stripe at the back of the helmet. These strips are lettered with each player's name.

2. Dallas wears silver-grey pants because original GM Tex Schramm saw the color in the interior of a rental car he was driving and fell in love with it. He ordered dye in the same color to create the pants and used it to pair with the Cowboys' white jerseys at home.

3. Cowboys Hall of Fame tackle and tight end Rayfield Wright wore numbers 67, 70, and 85 with Dallas. Each time coach Tom Landry shifted his position, Wright needed to shift numbers as well to conform with NFL rules.

4. The Philadelphia Eagles hosted the 1980 NFC Championship game against the Cowboys. The Eagles, against their own tradition, chose to wear white, because it forced Dallas to wear their "cursed" blue jerseys. The Eagles won the game 20-7 and advanced to the Super Bowl, which elevated the animosity between the rival teams.

5. Number 11 is popular with the Cowboys and has been worn by players at four positions: quarterback, kicker, wide receiver, and defensive back. QB Danny White and WR Cole Beasley were the most acclaimed players to wear it.

6. The blue star logo of the Dallas Cowboys is among the most iconic in all of sports. The star represents Texas

being the "Lone Star State," and blue was chosen because the AFL Dallas Texans (who were created during the same year) had chosen red for their uniforms. The star has remained unchanged since 1964.

7. Since 1973, the NFL no longer allows players to wear jersey number 0 or 00. No Dallas Cowboy ever wore either number in the 14 seasons prior to this change, so neither number will be used in franchise history.

8. While Dallas refuses to retire jersey numbers, they do have several that are out of circulation as a sign of respect for players such as Troy Aikman, Bob Lilly, Emmitt Smith, Roger Staubach, and others. This traditionally happens for players who enter the Cowboys Ring of Honor.

9. Cowboys away jerseys do not use the same blue as their home jerseys. Owner Jerry Jones wanted to maintain a classic home look "like the New York Yankees," so he has steadfastly had the team wear royal blue at home. The marketing team realized that navy blue sold much better in retail, so Jones allowed the team to switch to navy jerseys on the road.

10. Wide receiver Antonio Bryant had an incident with head coach Bill Parcells involving his jersey. Upset with his playing time, Bryant threw his jersey to the ground in frustration. Parcells grabbed it and threw it back at Bryant. Bryant then tossed the jersey into his coach's face. Following the incident, Bryant was unsurprisingly traded, to the Cleveland Browns.

CHAPTER 3:

COWBOYS QUARTERBACKS

QUIZ TIME!

1. In 1971, Roger Staubach eventually won the starting job in a mid-season quarterback controversy. He eventually led the Cowboys to their first Super Bowl Championship, but which quarterback did he take the starting job from?

   a. Craig Morton
   b. Don Meredith
   c. Gary Hogeboom
   d. Jerry Rhome

2. Tony Romo holds the top 4 spots on the Cowboys all-time list of most passing touchdowns thrown in a season.

   a. True
   b. False

3. Which quarterback has thrown the most interceptions in Dallas Cowboys franchise history?

   a. Craig Morton
   b. Danny White

c. Troy Aikman

   d. Eddie LeBaron

4. Which of these Cowboys quarterbacks has been sacked by opponents the most times during the span of their career (a total of 313 times sacked)?

   a. Tony Romo

   b. Jon Kitna

   c. Matt Cassell

   d. Roger Staubach

5. Which Dallas Cowboys quarterback is a strong enough golfer to have played in multiple PGA Tour events?

   a. Troy Aikman

   b. Tony Romo

   c. Danny White

   d. Kellen Moore

6. Cowboys quarterback Tony Romo was part of a military family that moved frequently. What city was his father stationed in when Romo was born?

   a. San Francisco, CA

   b. San Diego, CA

   c. Pittsburgh, PA

   d. Boston, MA

7. Troy Aikman has played more games at QB for the Cowboys than any other player.

   a. True

   b. False

8. Who is the Dallas Cowboys all-time career leader in most passing yards?

   a. Tony Romo
   b. Roger Staubach
   c. Dak Prescott
   d. Danny White

9. What is current Cowboys quarterback Dak Prescott's actual first name?

   a. Dakota
   b. Derek
   c. Adam
   d. Rayne

10. Which of these Cowboys quarterbacks went on to be a popular and frequently amusing commentator on *Monday Night Football* after his playing career ended?

    a. Don Meredith
    b. Danny White
    c. Jason Garrett
    d. Jon Kitna

11. Which of these Dallas Cowboys quarterbacks set the record for most passing yards thrown in Orange Bowl history with 453 yards? This record still stands today.

    a. Dak Prescott
    b. Troy Aikman
    c. Danny White
    d. Quincy Carter

12. Among quarterbacks who have played at least one season with Dallas, Eddie LeBaron has the highest interception percentage, with 7.7% of his passes thrown being picked off.

    a. True
    b. False

13. Tony Romo botched the hold on an extra point attempt in a very close 2007 playoff game against this team, causing an abrupt end to the Cowboys season and much negative media attention.

    a. Atlanta Falcons
    b. Philadelphia Eagles
    c. Seattle Seahawks
    d. New York Giants

14. Which of these Dallas Cowboys quarterbacks appeared as himself on an episode of Fox's long-running animated sitcom *The Simpsons*?

    a. Tony Romo
    b. Troy Aikman
    c. Roger Staubach
    d. Don Meredith

15. Joe Montana famously threw a game-winning touchdown to Dwight Clark in the San Francisco 49ers defeat of the Cowboys in the 1981 NFC Championship game. Who was the quarterback for the Cowboys in this game?

    a. Steve Pelluer
    b. Bernie Kosar

c. Glenn Carano

d. Danny White

16. Troy Aikman has won both a College Football National Championship and multiple NFL Super Bowl Championships.

    a. True

    b. False

17. Much like former head coach Jason Garrett, Kellen Moore was also a Cowboys quarterback at one point and is now coaching. What is Kellen Moore's title with the Dallas Cowboys?

    a. Defensive Coordinator

    b. Offensive Coordinator

    c. Wide Receivers Coach

    d. Quarterbacks Coach

18. As a commentator on *Monday Night Football*, what was Don Meredith's signature line?

    a. "That's all she wrote. Get your car keys out, folks!"

    b. "The place is here, the time is now…it's *Monday Night Football!*"

    c. "Let's get ready to rumble!"

    d. "Turn out the lights; the party's over!"

19. In 2019, Dak Prescott came within one yard of tying the Cowboys all-time single season passing yardage record. Who holds the record he fell just short of?

    a. Vinny Testaverde

b. Tony Romo

c. Troy Aikman

d. Kellen Moore

20. Cowboys QB Troy Aikman named previous QB Roger Staubach as the godfather when his daughter Jordan was born in 2001.

a. True

b. False

QUIZ ANSWERS

1. A – Craig Morton

2. A – True

3. C – Troy Aikman

4. D – Roger Staubach

5. B – Tony Romo

6. B – San Diego, CA

7. B – False

8. A – Tony Romo

9. D – Rayne

10. A – Don Meredith

11. A – Dak Prescott

12. A – True

13. C – Seattle Seahawks

14. B – Troy Aikman

15. D – Danny White

16. A – True

17. B – Offensive Coordinator

18. D – "Turn out the lights; the party's over!"

19. B – Tony Romo

20. B – False

DID YOU KNOW?

1. Only two Cowboys who were not primarily quarterbacks have ever thrown for more than one touchdown pass in a season. Running back Dan Reeves tossed two in 1967, and another running back, Calvin Hill, matched the feat with two of his own in 1969.

2. Cowboys Hall of Fame quarterback Roger Staubach's rookie year began unusually late at the age of 27. The reason for this was because of Staubach's active duty in the Naval Academy. He volunteered for a one-year tour of duty in Vietnam and also played football for service teams for years until he eventually joined the Cowboys; even having access to the Cowboys' playbook in the meantime.

3. Many notable quarterbacks at the end of their careers have come to Dallas as backups, often because endorsement deals are better in Dallas than anywhere else. Famous names to cycle through town for a short period include Randall Cunningham, Vinny Testaverde, and Bernie Kosar.

4. Dallas wide receiver Dez Bryant attempted exactly one pass for the Cowboys in his career. In a game against the Detroit Lions, he found tight end Jason Witten open for a touchdown. Bryant maintains a 100% completion percentage for his career… Not bad!

5. No Cowboy quarterback has ever been able to complete 70% of his passes in a season. The most accurate was Tony Romo, who came the closest in 2014, when he hit 69.9%.

6. Don Meredith owns the longest passing play in Cowboys history. He dropped back and found speedy receiver Bob Hayes for a 95-yard touchdown toss that helped Dallas go on to defeat the rival Washington Redskins in a tight matchup, 31-30.

7. Cowboy QB Eddie LeBaron was a lieutenant in the United States Marine Corps. He played football for their team, the Quantico Marines Devil Dogs, but more impressively earned both a Purple Heart and a Bronze Star for his service in the Korean War.

8. Dallas has been blessed with success in finding franchise quarterbacks. In a span of 56 years, from 1960-2016, five players provided the Cowboys with unmatched stability: Don Meredith, Roger Staubach, Danny White, Troy Aikman, and Tony Romo. There was only one gap, a four-year period between Aikman and Romo from 2000-2004, where the team struggled to find an answer.

9. Roger Staubach could have used some better blocking when he became the Cowboys QB in 1969. His sack percentage was over 18% in three of the following four years; which is among the highest rates in Cowboys history.

10. Staubach had better fortune in a 1975 playoff game against the Minnesota Vikings. Down 4 points, with only

seconds left in the game, he unleashed a 50-yard throw to Drew Pearson for the winning score. Afterward, Staubach said he had fired the pass and "said a Hail Mary" for its success, thus coining the term that is popularly used today.

CHAPTER 4:

THE PASS CATCHERS

QUIZ TIME!

1. Before later joining the Cowboys, star wide receiver Terrell Owens infamously celebrated two touchdowns inside of the star logo at midfield. On his second attempt, he was tackled by a Cowboy who was not amused by Owens's antics. What was this player's name?

    a. DeMarcus Ware
    b. Darren Woodson
    c. Terence Newman
    d. George Teague

2. Dez Bryant had the most touchdowns in one season for any Cowboys receiver, when he caught 16 from Tony Romo in 2014.

    a. True
    b. False

3. Which Cowboys pass catcher once held world records in several sprint categories and was thought of as the world's fastest human?

a. Joey Galloway

b. Michael Gallup

c. Bob Hayes

d. Miles Austin

4. Dallas tight end Jay Novacek was elected to the Nebraska High School Sports Hall of Fame for his accomplishments in three sports. Which of the following was NOT a sport that he participated in?

a. Football

b. Swimming

c. Basketball

d. Pole vault

5. Who holds the all-time career franchise records for both receiving yardage and receptions for the Cowboys?

a. Jason Witten

b. Dez Bryant

c. Michael Irvin

d. Drew Pearson

6. How did Drew Pearson suffer the injury that put an end to his NFL career?

a. Suffered a concussion while being tackled out of bounds on a late hit

b. Shot in the leg during an armed robbery at the team's hotel

c. Fell asleep while driving and crashed his vehicle

d. Broke a vertebra while diving into shallow water on vacation

7. As a child, future Cowboys wide receiver Mike Renfro served as a ball boy for the team while his father Ray was part of the coaching staff.

   a. True
   b. False

8. Two Cowboys with at least 100 receptions have averaged 20 yards per catch over their careers. Which two have shown this amazing big play ability?

   a. Michael Irvin and Joey Galloway
   b. Drew Pearson and Jay Novacek
   c. Dez Bryant and Terrell Owens
   d. Bob Hayes and Alvin Harper

9. Jason Witten ranks second in NFL history in receptions by a tight end. Which esteemed TE does he trail for the record?

   a. Tony Gonzalez
   b. Antonio Gates
   c. Rob Gronkowski
   d. Ozzie Newsome

10. In 1998, star wide receiver Michael Irvin was involved in a nasty physical altercation with a teammate in the Cowboys' locker room. What weapon did he use to attack that teammate, causing serious injury?

    a. Gun
    b. Baseball Bat
    c. Scissors
    d. Barbell Rack

11. Which Cowboys receiver released his own rap album titled *The Autobiography*, and also started his own record label called ColdNation Records?

    a. Dez Bryant

    b. Deion Sanders

    c. Alvin Harper

    d. Cole Beasley

12. In the early 2000s, wide receiver Terry Glenn played for Dallas along with two other key figures he had been with in New England: coach Bill Parcells and QB Drew Bledsoe.

    a. True

    b. False

13. Three pass catchers have over 500 career receptions for the Dallas Cowboys. Which of the following players is NOT among that club?

    a. Michael Irvin

    b. Drew Pearson

    c. Dez Bryant

    d. Jason Witten

14. From which rival team did the Cowboys poach star wide receiver Terrell Owens as a free agent in 2006?

    a. Philadelphia Eagles

    b. San Francisco 49ers

    c. New York Giants

    d. Buffalo Bills

15. Despite all his accomplishments, Bob Hayes has more career fumbles than any other Cowboys wide receiver. How many times did he cough up the ball?

    a. 11
    b. 15
    c. 17
    d. 22

16. The 1979 Cowboys were the first team in the NFL to have two 1,000-yard receivers (Drew Pearson and Tony Hill), AND a 1,000-yard rusher (Tony Dorsett) in their offense.

    a. True
    b. False

17. Amari Cooper signed the highest contract ever given out by Dallas to a wide receiver. How much was his contract worth?

    a. $70 million
    b. $80 million
    c. $90 million
    d. $100 million

18. What did Hall of Fame wide receiver Terrell Owens famously pour over his helmet as part of a touchdown celebration?

    a. Peanuts
    b. Popcorn
    c. Beer
    d. Cracker Jacks

19. Fan favorite Miles Austin was beloved for his underdog status. The undrafted free agent thrived with the Cowboys and made it to how many Pro Bowls?

    a. 0
    b. 1
    c. 2
    d. 3

20. WR Terrance Williams saw his playing time increase in 2016 after performing the Heimlich maneuver on coach Jason Garrett when the coach was choking on a donut.

    a. True
    b. False

QUIZ ANSWERS

1. D – George Teague

2. A – True

3. C – Bob Hayes

4. B – Swimming

5. A – Jason Witten

6. C – Fell asleep while driving and crashed his vehicle

7. A – True

8. D – Bob Hayes and Alvin Harper

9. A – Tony Gonzalez

10. C – Scissors

11. D – Cole Beasley

12. A – True

13. B – Drew Pearson

14. A – Philadelphia Eagles

15. C – 17

16. A – True

17. D – $100 million

18. B – Popcorn

19. C – 2

20. B – False

DID YOU KNOW?

1. Tight end Jason Witten retired from the Dallas Cowboys in 2018 to become a broadcaster in the *Monday Night Football* booth. The transition was not well-received by the viewing public, and Witten returned to the field for the grateful Cowboys in 2019.

2. Billy Joe Dupree got on the field for Dallas and refused to come off. He played every single game for 11 seasons in a distinguished career that was book-ended by two other excellent Cowboy tight ends; Mike Ditka before him and Doug Cosbie afterward.

3. The Cowboys leaderboard for receiving touchdowns is remarkably close at the top. Dez Bryant sits at the top with 73. He is one ahead of Jason Witten, who has 72. In third place is Bob Hayes, with 71.

4. In 1991, Dallas was poised to select receiver Rocket Ismail with the 1st overall pick in the entry draft. Ismail signed a record-breaking contract to play with the Toronto Argonauts of the CFL instead, where he starred in a championship season for them. Eight years later, the Cowboys finally did sign Ismail, after Michael Irvin suffered a career-ending injury.

5. Deep threat Bob Hayes was so fast and difficult to cover, that his speed led to the development of new defensive tactics that are still practiced today, such as the zone defense and bump-and-run coverage.

6. Dallas receiver Mike Renfro was the Cowboys MVP in 1985, but in 1987, when NFL players went on strike, Renfro crossed the picket line and played with the replacement players. When the real players came back in 1988, Renfro was cut by the team and never played anywhere in the league again.

7. In a 2014 divisional round playoff game against the Green Bay Packers, Cowboys star wide receiver Dez Bryant caught a crucial fourth quarter pass from Tony Romo but did not retain possession of the ball while extending for the end zone. It was ruled incomplete and ultimately ended the Cowboys' season. The call was so controversial that the rule was since changed by the NFL to allow for that circumstance to be ruled a catch.

8. Drew Pearson started with the Cowboys, but has also had a very successful life afterwards. Among other things, he has become a broadcaster, CEO of his own headwear company, a coach, a general manager, and a motivational speaker. For his achievements, he was awarded the NFL Alumni Career Achievement Award in 2005.

9. Michael Irvin's 1995 season was one for the record books. He caught 111 passes on 165 targets, for 1,603 yards (all Dallas records). Against the San Francisco 49ers, he also broke the NFC Championship game record with 192 receiving yards, but gave up a costly fumble as the Cowboys lost the chance to play in the Super Bowl.

10. Receiver Butch Johnson debuted his "California Quake"

touchdown celebration in 1981. It involved pretending to draw and fire guns, and was one of the reasons the NFL started policies to prohibit rehearsed celebrations and signs of violence on the field.

CHAPTER 5:

RUNNING WILD

QUIZ TIME!

1. At the beginning of the 2014 season, Cowboys rusher DeMarco Murray ran for over 100 yards in a streak of eight straight games to set an NFL record. Whose record did he break?

    a. Earl Campbell
    b. Jim Brown
    c. Thurman Thomas
    d. LaDainian Tomlinson

2. In 1968, running back Don Perkins requested that the Cowboys end the procedure of segregation at hotels on the road, and players of mixed races began to room together.

    a. True
    b. False

3. Who holds the Cowboys single-season franchise rushing yardage record after racking up 1,845 yards?

    a. Herschel Walker

b. Ezekiel Elliott

c. Emmitt Smith

d. DeMarco Murray

4. Four running backs have led the NFL in rushing for 3 or more consecutive seasons. Emmitt Smith is one. Which of these running backs has NOT joined him?

   a. Steve Van Buren

   b. Adrian Peterson

   c. Earl Campbell

   d. Jim Brown

5. Which running back has accumulated the most carries for Dallas without ever scoring a rushing touchdown?

   a. Robert Thomas

   b. Lance Dunbar

   c. Don Perkins

   d. James Jones

6. Dallas running back Julius Jones and Chicago Bears running back Thomas Jones became the first pair of brothers in the NFL to do what?

   a. Face each other in a game that was played on Thanksgiving Day

   b. Score four total rushing touchdowns in a single game

   c. Rush for 1,000 yards each in the same season

   d. Donate half of their salaries to charity for one full season

7. Fullback Amos Marsh once played slide trombone in a marching band at Texas Stadium as a teenager before he later made the Cowboys as an undrafted free agent.

   a. True
   b. False

8. Which two Cowboy running backs shared the backfield together in Dallas after having both won the Heisman Trophy for separate teams in college?

   a. Marion Barber and Julius Jones
   b. Don Perkins and Calvin Hill
   c. Ezekiel Elliott and Darren McFadden
   d. Tony Dorsett and Herschel Walker

9. How many running backs have carried the ball over 1,000 times for the Cowboys?

   a. 3
   b. 7
   c. 12
   d. 16

10. No Cowboys running back has averaged over 100 yards per game during his career. Ezekiel Elliott is the closest; what is his average?

   a. 92 yards/game
   b. 94.5 yards/game
   c. 96.5 yards/game
   d. 99 yards/game

11. In which season did Felix Jones record an astonishing 5.9 yards per carry for Dallas?

    a. 2008
    b. 2009
    c. 2010
    d. 2011

12. The football stadium at Hopewell High School, where Cowboys running back Tony Dorsett went to school, was renamed and is now called Tony Dorsett Stadium.

    a. True
    b. False

13. Which Dallas running back (with at least 300 carries) has the highest career yards gained per attempt, with 4.9?

    a. Felix Jones
    b. Duane Thomas
    c. DeMarco Murray
    d. Emmitt Smith

14. On the Cowboys leaderboard for most rushing touchdowns in a season, how many times does an Emmitt Smith season appear in the top 10 entries?

    a. 2
    b. 4
    c. 6
    d. 10

15. In which sport did Dallas RB Herschel Walker qualify for the 1992 Winter Olympic games in Albertville, France?

a. Speed skating

b. Bobsled

c. Alpine skiing

d. Biathlon

16. Emmitt Smith has 153 rushing touchdowns with the Cowboys, which is more than the next three highest Dallas running backs combined.

   a. True

   b. False

17. Defensive teammates described attempting to tackle small but tough fullback Robert Newhouse in practice as:

   a. "Like wrapping your arms around a mad grizzly bear"

   b. "Like letting a garbage truck run you over… repeatedly"

   c. "Like trying to tackle a fire hydrant"

   d. "Like squaring up to catch a swinging wrecking ball"

18. Which Dallas running back has the most career fumbles?

   a. Emmitt Smith

   b. Tony Dorsett

   c. Calvin Hill

   d. Walt Garrison

19. Which Cowboy had the highest single season rushing yards per game, with 115.3?

   a. Tony Dorsett

   b. Herschel Walker

c. Ezekiel Elliott

d. DeMarco Murray

20. Fullback Walt Garrison led the Cowboys in receptions for their 1971 championship-winning season, despite the presence of two Hall of Fame wide receivers and a Hall of Fame tight end on the roster.

a. True

b. False

QUIZ ANSWERS

1. B – Jim Brown

2. A – True

3. D – DeMarco Murray

4. B – Adrian Peterson

5. A – Robert Thomas

6. C – Rush for 1,000 yards each in the same season

7. B – False

8. D – Tony Dorsett and Herschel Walker

9. B – 7

10. C – 96.5 yards/game

11. B – 2009

12. A – True

13. B – Duane Thomas

14. C – 6

15. B – Bobsled

16. B – False

17. C – "Like trying to tackle a fire hydrant"

18. B – Tony Dorsett

19. D – DeMarco Murray

20. A – True

DID YOU KNOW?

1. Don Perkins was the first running back to sign with the Dallas Cowboys (which he did even before the franchise was created). But, due to an injury, he missed their first season, and Don McIlhenny became the first fullback to actually play for them.

2. When not starting for the Dallas Cowboys, fullback Walt Garrison was a real cowboy who participated in professional rodeos during his offseason. While he did not make the Pro Football Hall of Fame, Garrison *is* a member of the Texas Cowboy Hall of Fame.

3. Tony Dorsett holds the record for the longest touchdown ever scored for the Dallas Cowboys. He broke free for the 99-yard score in front of many prime-time viewers, during *Monday Night Football* on January 3, 1983, against the Minnesota Vikings.

4. Legendary running back Emmitt Smith leads not only the Dallas Cowboys in career rushing yards, but also the entire NFL. He is the only man to break 17,000 yards on the ground.

5. Cowboys running back Marion Barber III was part of a very athletic football family. His father, Marion Jr., was a running back for the New York Jets. One brother, Dominique, was a safety for the Houston Texans, and another, Thomas, played for the Minnesota Golden

Gophers. In addition, his cousin, Peyton, is a running back for the Tampa Bay Buccaneers.

6. Decorated franchise icon Tony Dorsett is one of only two people to: win a Heisman Trophy, win a College National Championship, win a Super Bowl, be elected to the College Football Hall of Fame, and be elected to the Pro Football Hall of Fame. Marcus Allen is the other.

7. Running back Calvin Hill won the 1969 NFL Rookie of the Year Award, but is not the most acclaimed athlete in his family. His son, Grant Hill, won the 1995 NBA Rookie of the Year Award and is an inductee of the Basketball Hall of Fame.

8. In a 2016 Sunday night game against the Tampa Bay Buccaneers, All-Pro running back Ezekiel Elliott famously jumped into an oversized Salvation Army bucket after scoring a touchdown. He was flagged and fined by the NFL for excessive celebration, however, the Salvation Army reported a massive spike in donations, totaling over $180k in the 24 hours following Zeke's stunt.

9. Emmitt Smith has appeared on several TV shows, including *How I Met Your Mother*, *Deal or No Deal*, *Dancing with the Stars*, and *The Miss Universe Pageant*.

10. Dallas RB Herschel Walker was quite the athletic specimen. In addition to his NFL career and Olympic qualification in bobsled, he is also a 5th degree black belt in Tae Kwon Do, and has danced with a professional ballet company in Texas.

CHAPTER 6:

IN THE TRENCHES

QUIZ TIME!

1. Two Cowboys defenders have recorded 5 sacks in a single game. Which two were they?

    a. DeMarcus Lawrence and DeMarcus Ware
    b. Bob Lilly and Jim Jeffcoat
    c. Greg Ellis and Randy White
    d. Tony Tolbert and Charles Haley

2. Cowboys defensive linemen Larry Cole and Pat Toomay, along with guard Blaine Nye, rebelled against some of the flashier members of the team by founding The Zero Club, whose motto was "Thou Shalt Not Seek Publicity."

    a. True
    b. False

3. The Patriots' Tom Brady recently broke the record for most Super Bowl wins, with 6. Which Cowboys defensive end had previously held the record, with 5?

    a. Tony Tolbert
    b. Bob Lilly

c. Charles Haley

d. Dexter Coakley

4. Who is the Cowboys all-time franchise leader in sacks with 117?

   a. Ed Jones

   b. DeMarcus Lawrence

   c. Greg Ellis

   d. DeMarcus Ware

5. The 6'3", 325-pound guard Larry Allen is perhaps the most powerful man to ever play for the Cowboys. In his prime, how much was he officially able to bench press?

   a. 500 pounds

   b. 585 pounds

   c. 650 pounds

   d. 705 pounds

6. Dallas guard Zack Martin was a teammate and roommate of which current Cincinnati Bengal player while they were at Notre Dame, before the player married his sister and the two became brothers-in-law?

   a. Joe Mixon

   b. Tyler Eifert

   c. A.J. Green

   d. Geno Atkins

7. The 2013 Dallas Cowboys hold the NFL record for the heaviest combined weight of all starting offensive and defensive linemen.

a. True

b. False

8. Which decorated Cowboys defensive lineman won three Super Bowls to go along with his two college National Championships?

    a. Russell Maryland
    b. DeMarcus Lawrence
    c. Randy White
    d. Jim Jeffcoat

9. Dallas guard Nate Newton *loved* to eat. He ate so much that at his favorite restaurant (a deli near the Cowboys' stadium), he had not one but three meals named after him. Which of the following was NOT actually on their menu?

    a. The Nate's Special
    b. The Double N Burger
    c. The Newton Ultimate
    d. The Newton Extra

10. Which Cowboy defender showed the best nose for the ball, by leading the team in most career forced fumbles?

    a. DeMarcus Lawrence
    b. Jim Jeffcoat
    c. Greg Ellis
    d. DeMarcus Ware

11. Two members of the Dallas defensive line, DeMarcus Lawrence and Tyrone Crawford, travel to Cowboy home games in this unique manner:

a. Riding bicycles together

b. Getting a ride with their mothers

c. Taking the city bus

d. Jet skiing down the nearby river

12. A contract dispute over offensive tackle Ralph Neely between the Cowboys and the AFL Houston Oilers led to the creation of the Governor's Cup—a preseason game between the teams—when the AFL merged with the NFL in 1966.

a. True

b. False

13. Which current member of the Cowboys' vaunted offensive line has been an offensive captain of the team for the past two seasons?

a. Travis Frederick

b. Tyron Smith

c. Zack Martin

d. La'el Collins

14. Coach Tom Landry once said glowingly of which defensive player: "His performances range from spectacular to spectacular."

a. Randy White

b. Ed Jones

c. Bob Lilly

d. Harvey Martin

15. Michael Strahan, a pass rusher for the rival New York Giants, so respected which Dallas offensive lineman that

he mentioned the lineman specifically in his Pro Football Hall of Fame induction speech.

   a. Mark Tuinei

   b. Erik Williams

   c. Mark Stepnoski

   d. Kevin Gogan

16. In his youth, Cowboys tackle Mark Tuinei played on the same basketball team in Hawaii as future U.S. president, Barack Obama.

   a. True

   b. False

17. Talented defensive lineman Leon Lett was a force for the Cowboys when he was on the field, but he was frequently suspended for substance abuse violations. How many games did Lett miss due to suspension?

   a. 8

   b. 12

   c. 15

   d. 28

18. Three quarterbacks top the record books for most fumbles recovered by the Cowboys, but they tend to clean up their own mess. Which defender has created the most turnovers for Dallas by recovering an opponent's fumble?

   a. Cliff Harris

   b. Too Tall Jones

   c. DeMarcus Ware

   d. Bob Lilly

19. Standout Cowboys center Travis Frederick was forced to retire from the NFL in 2020, after missing a full season, due to what medical cause?

   a. Diabetes
   b. Guillain-Barre syndrome
   c. Cirrhosis of the liver
   d. Multiple sclerosis

20. Bob Lilly capitalized on the misfortune of opponents more than any other Cowboy, by scoring three career touchdowns on fumble returns.

   a. True
   b. False

QUIZ ANSWERS

1. B – Bob Lilly and Jim Jeffcoat

2. A – True

3. C – Charles Haley

4. D – DeMarcus Ware

5. D – 705 pounds

6. B – Tyler Eifert

7. B – False

8. A – Russell Maryland

9. B – The Double N Burger

10. D – DeMarcus Ware

11. A – Riding bicycles together

12. A – True

13. C – Zack Martin

14. A – Randy White

15. B – Erik Williams

16. A – True

17. D – 28

18. B – Too Tall Jones

19. B – Guillain-Barre syndrome

20. A – True

DID YOU KNOW?

1. Franchise legend Bob Lilly ran a profitable alcoholic beverage business after his retirement from the Cowboys. However, he was a man of such morals that he gave up the business entirely after viewing a drunk-driving accident involving his product, and took up photography instead.

2. Cowboys DE Ed Jones appeared as a guest referee at WrestleMania 2 in Chicago for a 20-man battle royale between wrestlers and NFL players (including fellow Cowboy Harvey Martin). Andre the Giant was crowned the winner of the match.

3. Although he was also drafted by the AFL's Oakland Raiders, defensive tackle Jethro Pugh chose to play with the Cowboys...and only the Cowboys. He spent his entire 14-year NFL career with the team, good for the fourth longest tenure in franchise history.

4. Three defensive linemen share the Dallas record for most safeties created. John Dutton, Harvey Martin, and Jethro Pugh all recorded two (as did cornerback Benny Barnes).

5. Defensive tackle Randy White was extremely tough, competed in Thai boxing, and once beat up rebellious teammate Hollywood Henderson in a locker room scuffle. But he also had a soft spot for animals, and once smuggled a stray dog onto a plane so it would not be put down at the local pound.

6. Center Mark Stepnoski had an excellent career with Dallas, including five Pro Bowls and two Super Bowls. But his public support for the legalization of marijuana actually got him kicked *out* of his high school's (Cathedral Preparatory School) Hall of Fame.

7. Defensive end Tony Tolbert had more sacks than any other Cowboy during the 1990s, but his career could have been even better if not for injuries. Tolbert endured seven knee surgeries in nine years, and had both knees replaced upon his retirement.

8. Larry Cole, a defensive lineman, played for the Cowboys from 1968 through 1981, becoming the first Dallas player to appear for the team in three different decades.

9. Offensive lineman Rayfield Wright may be one of the most decorated Cowboys ever. He is a member of both the Texas and Georgia Sports Halls of Fame, the Pro Football Hall of Fame, the State of Georgia Hall of Fame, and several other distinctions, including the Dallas Cowboys Ring of Honor.

10. The 2002 Dallas Cowboys were the first NFL team in history to start five African-American players on the offensive line. These players included Flozell Adams, Solomon Page, Kelvin Garmon, Larry Allen, and Andre Gurode.

CHAPTER 7:

THE BACK SEVEN

QUIZ TIME!

1. Dallas linebacker Ken Norton Jr.'s father was more famous than his son, because of what reason?

   a. Winning two Academy Awards for his sound editing work

   b. Being the heavyweight boxing champion of the world

   c. Helping to recue 43 hostages during a standoff in a terrorist attack

   d. Being elected to office as a three-time California senator

2. Terence Newman played cornerback for three NFL teams, and Mike Zimmer coached him in all three locations.

   a. True

   b. False

3. Which former Dallas cornerback became a defensive coach in the NFL, helping turn fellow CBs Darrelle Revis and Stephon Gilmore into All-Pro players?

a. Larry Brown

b. Orlando Scandrick

c. Terence Newman

d. Dennis Thurman

4. Which Cowboys cornerback is the franchise's all-time leader in interceptions with 52?

a. Everson Walls

b. Chidobe Awuzie

c. Mel Renfro

d. Terence Newman

5. Which former Dallas cornerback now hosts pregame and postgame shows on the Cowboys' flagship radio station?

a. Kevin Smith

b. Larry Brown

c. Deion Sanders

d. Ron Francis

6. Hard-hitting safety Cliff Harris wore placekicker pads so he could be faster in pursuit of ball-carriers. Cowboys coach George Allen once colorfully described him as:

a. "A rolling ball of butcher knives"

b. "A tenacious son of a gun who'll track you down like a posse earning a bounty"

c. "A one-man wolfpack that hasn't eaten in three days"

d. "A week of painkillers waiting to happen"

7. During the 2010s' poker craze, members of Dallas's secondary and linebacking corps held a weekly game

where, rather than playing for money, the losers had to tweet embarrassing things about themselves or flattering things about the winners.

   a. True

   b. False

8. Although sacks are usually not a high priority for defensive backs in most coaching systems, one Cowboys DB excelled at this skill, putting up 18 sacks in his career. Who?

   a. Bill Bates

   b. Orlando Scandrick

   c. Terence Newman

   d. Michael Downs

9. Two Cowboys players share the team's lead for most interceptions returned for a touchdown, with 4 apiece. Who are they?

   a. Deion Sanders and Cornell Green

   b. Mel Renfro and Everson Walls

   c. Lee Roy Jordan and Roy Williams

   d. Dennis Thurman and Dexter Coakley

10. This middle linebacker was usually the smallest in the NFL, at only 6'1" and 220 pounds, but he was a longtime Cowboys standout who made five Pro Bowls.

   a. Sean Lee

   b. Lee Roy Jordan

   c. Dexter Coakley

   d. Chuck Howley

11. Although he quickly got over it after being drafted by Dallas, Darren Woodson has admitted that he "couldn't stand the Cowboys" as a kid. Which NFL team was he a fan of?

    a. Washington Redskins
    b. Arizona Cardinals
    c. Pittsburgh Steelers
    d. Philadelphia Eagles

12. Cowboys DB Byron Jones has interned with two members of the United States government as part of his college program requirements.

    a. True
    b. False

13. This player led the Cowboys in interceptions for five seasons, and led the NFL in interceptions for three seasons, both of which are records.

    a. Darren Woodson
    b. Everson Walls
    c. Cliff Harris
    d. Byron Jones

14. Which Cowboys player won NFL Special Teams Player of the Year both of his first two years in the league, and retired as their all-time leader in special team tackles?

    a. Darren Woodson
    b. Dat Nyguen
    c. Dexter Coakley
    d. Bill Bates

15. Defensive back Everson Walls felt such a strong bond for his Cowboys teammates that he donated a kidney to one of them. Which teammate's life did he save?

    a. Drew Pearson
    b. Harvey Martin
    c. Ron Springs
    d. Tony Dorsett

16. Former Cowboys safety Charlie Waters became a CBS broadcaster, but was fired after saying of one team in a promo shoot: "They have a collective IQ of about 40."

    a. True
    b. False

17. Which Cowboy unofficially leads the team with the most career tackles, with approximately 130 more than his nearest competition?

    a. Charles Haley
    b. Ken Norton
    c. Tony Tolbert
    d. Darren Woodson

18. Linebacker Hollywood Henderson had such an impressive mix of skill and flamboyance that this future Hall of Fame linebacker admitted to modelling Henderson's game and wore his number.

    a. Ray Lewis
    b. Brian Urlacher
    c. Mike Singletary
    d. Lawrence Taylor

19. The most consecutive seasons in which a single player has led the Cowboys in tackles is six. Which player accomplished this feat?

    a. Sean Lee
    b. Bradie James
    c. Terence Newman
    d. Larry Brown

20. Dallas linebacker Chuck Howley lettered in five sports at West Virginia University, including wrestling, football, swimming, track, and gymnastics. He was also a diver, but did not letter in the sport.

    a. True
    b. False

QUIZ ANSWERS

1. B – Being the heavyweight boxing champion of the world

2. A – True

3. D – Dennis Thurman

4. C – Mel Renfro

5. B – Larry Brown

6. A – "A rolling ball of butcher knives"

7. B – False

8. A – Bill Bates

9. D – Dennis Thurman and Dexter Coakley

10. B – Lee Roy Jordan

11. C – Pittsburgh Steelers

12. A – True

13. B – Everson Walls

14. D – Bill Bates

15. C – Ron Springs

16. B – False

17. D – Darren Woodson

18. D – Lawrence Taylor

19. B – Bradie James

20. A – True

DID YOU KNOW?

1. Safety Mel Renfro was such an impressive athlete that after being named an All-Pro in 1965, the Cowboys moved him to running back to jumpstart the offense the following year. An injury in his first game pre-empted that move, so he went back to being an All-Pro safety, before eventually moving to cornerback and earning All-Pro honors there as well.

2. D.D. Lewis, who started at linebacker for the Cowboys, was born in 1945 and was the youngest of 14 children. His parents had used up all of their favorite names by this point, so he was named after two great American World War II Generals, Dwight Eisenhower and Douglas McArthur.

3. Cornerback Bryan McCann set the Cowboys record for longest interception returned for a touchdown, in only his second NFL game. Against the New York Giants, he grabbed an Eli Manning pass in the end zone and ran it back 101 yards. The following week against Detroit, the rookie ran a punt back 97 yards for a touchdown, which netted him NFC Defensive Player of the Week and NFC Special Teams Player of the Week, back to back.

4. One of a kind Deion Sanders was not just a shutdown cornerback for the Cowboys. He also played professional baseball, appearing in both the Super Bowl and the World

Series. Sanders demonstrated his impact in many ways, and once scored a touchdown and hit a home run in the same week.

5. In 2008, the Cowboys had two players with the same name: Roy Williams. Both had been 1st round picks, and both had been to the Pro Bowl. One played safety for the team, and the other played wide receiver, which meant that they often practiced directly against each other.

6. Passes defended is a stat that the NFL began using at the turn of the century. Cornerback Terence Newman has dominated the statistic for the Cowboys, having almost twice as many as his closest competition (Orlando Scandrick).

7. When Joe Montana hit Dwight Clark in the end zone for "The Catch" that led the San Francisco 49ers to victory over Dallas in the 1982 NFL Championship, DB Everson Walls was pictured in the famous photo trying to defend the pass. Clark approached Walls at a banquet later and told him to get in touch with Kodak to be compensated for the photo. Walls had no idea this was possible, and he and Clark remained friends for years afterward.

8. Jack Del Rio is one of the more well-traveled men in the NFL. In addition to playing linebacker for the Cowboys, he also played with four other teams, and went on to coach for seven NFL franchises. Del Rio has appeared in every current NFL division except the NFC West.

9. Certain players stand out for not just talent, but for their

effort as well. Linebacker Sean Lee was one such player, and definitely led by example. His coach once said, "He plays so hard, the other kids know they have to play that way to stay in the game. I can't take him out!"

10. In 1993, Dallas started Larry Brown and Kevin Smith at the cornerback positions. The duo combined to create the youngest set of starting cornerbacks in the NFL.

CHAPTER 8:

ODDS & ENDS & AWARDS

QUIZ TIME!

1. The Cowboys are a major draw for fans, and began a sellout streak in 2002 that is still active. How many consecutive games (both home and away) have they sold out?

    a. 88
    b. 135
    c. 157
    d. 190

2. When accepting his Academy Award for *Forrest Gump*, Tom Hanks said in his speech, "Growing up, I always wanted to be the quarterback for the Dallas Cowboys, but I guess this is pretty good too."

    a. True
    b. False

3. Which Dallas front office member once famously said that the hole in the roof of Texas Stadium was there so that "God could watch his favorite team play"?

a. Jimmy Johnson
b. Tom Landry
c. D.D. Lewis
d. Jerry Jones

4. What negative event befell linebacker Greg Ellis before he returned to the Cowboys and won the 2007 Comeback Player of the Year Award?

a. He was diagnosed with testicular cancer.
b. He tore his Achilles tendon.
c. He lost his memory in a car accident.
d. He contracted the SARS virus.

5. On Tony Dorsett's historic 99-yard run in 1982, the Cowboys had only ten men on the field. Which player missed the call to participate in the play?

a. Fullback Ron Springs
b. Tackle Pat Donovan
c. Tight End Doug Cosbie
d. Wide Receiver Tony Hill

6. Who is the longest tenured head coach of the Dallas Cowboys?

a. Bill Parcells
b. Jason Garrett
c. Tom Landry
d. Jimmy Johnson

7. In addition to coaching the Dallas Cowboys, Jason Garrett had also previously played for the team.

a. True

b. False

8. What is Brad Sham's connection to the Dallas Cowboys?

    a. An architect who designed and built AT&T Stadium for the Cowboys

    b. A groundskeeper who has worked for the Cowboys since the 1970s

    c. A player agent who represented Tony Romo, Dez Bryant, and several others

    d. A radio announcer known as "the voice of the Cowboys"

9. Which Cowboys player is the only athlete in history to win both the Super Bowl and an Olympic gold medal?

    a. Larry Allen

    b. Bob Hayes

    c. Joey Galloway

    d. Deion Sanders

10. Only one Cowboys player has ever won the NFL's Defensive Player of the Year Award. Who took home that trophy?

    a. Harvey Martin

    b. Deion Sanders

    c. DeMarcus Ware

    d. Cliff Branch

11. In 1999, the last player to play for original Cowboys coach Tom Landry retired, after suffering a spinal cord injury against the Philadelphia Eagles. Who was it?

    a. Nate Newton

b. Jay Novacek

c. Michael Irvin

d. Kevin Smith

12. In retirement, former Dallas running back Herschel Walker started a shoe company which included a line of football footwear called "Cowboy Cleats."

a. True

b. False

13. Who was the first Dallas Cowboy to be elected to an All-Pro team by sportswriters?

a. Bob Hayes

b. Don Perkins

c. Frank Clarke

d. Bob Lilly

14. How many head coaches have roamed the sidelines for the Cowboys in their history?

a. 4

b. 9

c. 12

d. 16

15. Three Dallas head coaches have won the award as AP NFL Coach of the Year. Which of the following has never accomplished that?

a. Tom Landry

b. Jimmy Johnson

c. Barry Switzer

d. Jason Garrett

16. The Dallas Cowboys have the most wins of any franchise in NFL history.

    a. True
    b. False

17. Every Dallas head coach up to 2019 has led the team to the NFL playoffs, except for which one?

    a. Dave Campo
    b. Barry Switzer
    c. Chan Gailey
    d. Wade Phillips

18. Which fashion accessory was legendary head coach Tom Landry best known for wearing?

    a. Wristwatch
    b. Scarf
    c. Sunglasses
    d. Fedora

19. Only one Cowboy has ever been named the NFL's Offensive Player of the Year. Who received that honor?

    a. Emmitt Smith
    b. Ezekiel Elliott
    c. DeMarco Murray
    d. Tony Romo

20. When original general manager Tex Schramm passed away, he requested to have the words "Forever a Cowboy" inscribed on his tombstone.

    a. True
    b. False

QUIZ ANSWERS

1. D – 190

2. B – False

3. C – D.D. Lewis

4. B – He tore his Achilles tendon.

5. A – Fullback Ron Springs

6. C – Tom Landry

7. A – True

8. D – A radio announcer known as "the voice of the Cowboys"

9. B – Bob Hayes

10. A – Harvey Martin

11. C – Michael Irvin

12. B – False

13. B – Don Perkins

14. B – 9

15. C – Barry Switzer

16. B – False

17. A – Dave Campo

18. D – Fedora

19. C – DeMarco Murray

20. B – False

DID YOU KNOW?

1. The Dallas Cowboys are the only team in the NFL that chooses to wear white at home. Tex Schramm, former president and general manager of the Cowboys, decided the Cowboys should wear white at home so that Cowboys fans in attendance and on television, could see the various colors of the away teams each week. Some suggest that wearing white also helped in the Texas heat when the Cowboys played outdoors at Texas Stadium.

2. Remarkably, from 1966 until 1985, Dallas always fielded a winning team. Those 20 consecutive seasons above .500 are still an NFL record.

3. In 2007, the Cowboys set a new record by sending 13 of their players to Hawaii for the league's Pro Bowl.

4. Three Cowboys have won the NFL's Walter Payton Man of the Year Award. Roger Staubach was the first, in 1978. Troy Aikman won in 1997. And Jason Witten was the most recent winner, in 2012.

5. Head coach Bill Parcells came out of retirement in 2003 to coach the Dallas Cowboys. Well known for his unique approach, Parcells decided to strip the star logo from the helmets of all incoming rookies in training camp. He told them that they would have to prove themselves and earn the star. This has become tradition in Dallas and still to this day, rookies must first make the roster before the star is placed back onto their helmet.

6. Former coach Jimmy Johnson once appeared as a contestant on the reality TV show *Survivor*. Johnson was a big fan of the show, but was voted off the island on Day 8, finishing in 18th place. He called it "the toughest thing I've ever gone through."

7. Four Dallas Cowboys have won the Offensive Rookie of the Year Award (Calvin Hill, Tony Dorsett, Emmitt Smith, and Dak Prescott), but none have ever won the Defensive Rookie of the Year Award.

8. Cowboys coach Tom Landry roamed the Dallas sidelines for 28 years. In 1989, new owner Jerry Jones took over and fired Landry on his very first day in charge, feeling that the coach had lost touch with a different era of players.

9. Dallas has played the most playoff games of any NFL franchise (63). They are tied with the Green Bay Packers for 3rd in most playoff victories, behind the Pittsburgh Steelers and New England Patriots.

10. Emmitt Smith still holds the NFL's all-time record for career rushing yards with 18,355. He is the only Dallas Cowboy to have ever won NFL MVP of the regular season.

CHAPTER 9:

NICKNAMES

QUIZ TIME!

1. Which Dallas player is affectionately known by players and fans as "Mr. Cowboy"?

   a. Roger Staubach
   b. Bob Lilly
   c. Troy Aikman
   d. Tony Dorsett

2. Running back Amos "Forward" Marsh had no military experience. Instead, his moniker was given to him because of his powerful running style.

   a. True
   b. False

3. Why was Cowboys tight end Mike Ditka known around the league as "Iron Mike"?

   a. He was among the first to use weight rooms routinely, and had the muscles to show for it.
   b. When holding out for a higher contract, he refused to budge on his demands.

c. His vice-like handshake was by far the firmest on the team.

d. He was born and raised in a steel town in Pennsylvania.

4. The 1971 Dallas Cowboys, eventual winners of Super Bowl VI, had a fearsome defense that was known by this nickname:

    a. Hit Squad

    b. Doomsday Defense

    c. Steel Curtain

    d. OK Corral

5. Two rather large Cowboys of different eras were nicknamed "Big Cat" because of their surprising nimbleness at their size. Which two shared the nickname?

    a. Rayfield Wright and Leon Lett

    b. Ed Jones and Nate Newton

    c. Larry Allen and DeMarcus Ware

    d. Tyron Smith and Bob Lilly

6. Due to his fleetness and gracefulness, wide receiver Lance Alworth was known as what?

    a. The Gazelle

    b. Ballerina

    c. Lancelot

    d. Bambi

7. Defensive lineman Randy White was called "The Manster" because those who lined up against him thought he was "half man, half monster"?

a. True

b. False

8. Which Cowboy was known as "Moose" in recognition for his blocking prowess?

   a. Jay Novacek

   b. Daryl Johnston

   c. Jason Witten

   d. Rayfield Wright

9. Roger Staubach was known by quite a few different nicknames. Which of the following is NOT one of them?

   a. Roger the Dodger

   b. Captain America

   c. Iron Man

   d. Captain Comeback

10. Quarterback Danny White noticed the 1985 Dallas secondary (Michael Downs, Everson Walls, Ron Fellows, and Dennis Thurman) had racked up an impressive 33 interceptions, so he dubbed them this:

    a. Turnover on Downs

    b. Impassible Walls

    c. The Takeaway Fellows

    d. Thurman's Thieves

11. What was Dallas head coach Bill Parcells also known as?

    a. Smarty

    b. The Big Tuna

    c. The Owl

d. Old Ironsides

12. The 6'7" offensive tackle Flozell Adams checked into training camp at 335 pounds, and his size led him to be christened "Flozell The Hotel."

    a. True
    b. False

13. Wide receiver Drew Pearson went by which one-word nickname?

    a. Hands
    b. Snag
    c. Sizzle
    d. Clutch

14. This trio of Hall-of-Famers affectionately known by Cowboys fans as "The Triplets" won three Super Bowls together.

    a. Dak Prescott, Amari Cooper, and Ezekiel Elliot
    b. Tony Romo, Terrell Owens, and DeMarco Murray
    c. Troy Aikman, Emmitt Smith, and Michael Irvin
    d. Deion Sanders, Darren Woodson, and Larry Allen

15. Most NFL fans actually knew 6'9" defensive end Ed Jones better by which nickname?

    a. The Giant
    b. Too Tall
    c. Wilt
    d. Massive Man

16. Fullback Robert Newhouse was nicknamed "The Human Bowling Ball" because he knocked down and scattered would-be tacklers as if they were pins.

    a. True
    b. False

17. Sack specialist DeMarcus Lawrence was known to Cowboys fans by what military nickname?

    a. The Admiral
    b. Tank
    c. Blitzkrieg
    d. Warlord

18. Hall of Fame defensive back Cliff Harris was nicknamed what, because of his hard hits?

    a. Smash
    b. Captain Crash
    c. Mack Truck Harris
    d. The Annihilator

19. Due to his tendency to come up big in big situations, wide receiver Michael Irvin was known as this:

    a. Mike When It Matters Most
    b. Clutch
    c. Fourth Quarter
    d. The Playmaker

20. Team owner Jerry Jones is known by players as "Uncle Pennybags" in homage to the rich Monopoly mascot.

    a. True
    b. False

QUIZ ANSWERS

1. B – Bob Lilly

2. A – True

3. D – He was born and raised in a steel town in Pennsylvania.

4. B – Doomsday Defense

5. A – Rayfield Wright and Leon Lett

6. D – Bambi

7. A – True

8. B – Daryl Johnston

9. C – Iron Man

10. D – Thurman's Thieves

11. B – The Big Tuna

12. A – True

13. D – Clutch

14. C – Troy Aikman, Emmitt Smith, and Michael Irvin

15. B – Too Tall

16. A – True

17. B – Tank

18. B – Captain Crash

19. D – The Playmaker

20. B – False

DID YOU KNOW?

1. Dallas guard Zack Martin struck fear in the hearts of opponents when they found out that his nickname "The Butcher" had been earned as a basketball player. What, they wondered, would he do to them in a contact sport like football?

2. Wide receiver "Bullet" Bob Hayes earned his nickname as a world-class sprinter whose two Olympic gold medals proved that he was faster than a speeding bullet.

3. During the late 1970s, Dallas accumulated offensive linemen John Fitzgerald, Tom Rafferty, Herb Scott, Pat Donovan, and Jim Cooper. Their similar ancestry soon had them being referred to as "Four Irishmen and a Scott."

4. Deion Sanders came to the Cowboys with two nicknames. "Neon Deion" referred to his flashy personality and style of play. "Prime Time" was chosen because he made people tune in to watch him, like they would for popular television shows aired in the evening.

5. Bruce Carter, who played with Cowboys linebacker Sean Lee, named him "General Lee," in part because Lee was an excellent leader who called plays for the defense, and part after Civil War general Robert E. Lee.

6. Running back Marion Barber was known for his punishing running style and for being tough to bring

down. He was given the lyrical nickname "Marion the Barbarian."

7. Massive guard Nate Newton was often compared to the Chicago Bears' William "The Refrigerator" Perry. Since Newton was even bigger, teammates called him "The Kitchen."

8. Linebacker Thomas Henderson earned his well-known nickname from teammate Robert Newhouse. After showing up to practice in a limousine while wearing a fur coat, he was henceforth known as "Hollywood" Henderson.

9. In the early 1990s, the Cowboys offensive line featured excellent pass protectors in Nate Newton, Mark Tuinei, Erik Williams, Mark Stepnoski, and Kevin Gogan. The group came to be known as "The Great Wall of Dallas."

10. Cowboys phenomenon Raghib Ismail was nicknamed "The Rocket," partially for his explosive and dynamic playing style, and partially because it was close to what his Arabic name meant in English. Ismail's brothers Qadry and Sulaiman also played football, and were known as "The Missile" and "The Bomb."

CHAPTER 10:

ALMA MATERS

QUIZ TIME!

1. Cowboys superstar WR Michael Irvin referred to his school as "The U." Which school did he attend?

   a. Alabama

   b. Texas Tech

   c. Miami

   d. Penn State

2. Legendary guard Larry Allen made the Hall of Fame despite playing college football at a tiny school called Sonoma State.

   a. True

   b. False

3. Dallas quarterback Tony Romo came from which relatively small school that also produced three NFL head coaches?

   a. Texas Christian

   b. Bowling Green

c. San Diego State

d. Eastern Illinois

4. Star running back Calvin Hill attended which prestigious Ivy League school?

a. Princeton

b. Penn

c. Yale

d. Harvard

5. Who did the Cowboys select in 1974 as the first player ever drafted 1st overall to come out of a historically black college?

a. Harvey Martin

b. Ed Jones

c. Rayfield Wright

d. Jethro Pugh

6. Before being selected by the Cowboys in 2016, linebacker Jaylon Smith suffered a terrible knee injury in his last game for which college program?

a. Notre Dame

b. Purdue

c. Michigan

d. Nebraska

7. Because of the rivalry between the two states, the Cowboys have never drafted a player from the University of Oklahoma.

a. True

b. False

8. The University of Buffalo has only had 15 players drafted into the NFL. Dallas took one of them, who suited up for 52 games for the Cowboys. Who was he?

    a. DB Josh Thomas
    b. WR Dwayne Harris
    c. OT Sam Young
    d. LB Victor Butler

9. Stud running back Ezekiel Elliott helped "dot the i" at which formidable college football program?

    a. Florida State University
    b. Ohio State University
    c. University of California Los Angeles
    d. Michigan State University

10. Which Cowboys draft pick was a fighter pilot out of the Air Force who flew missions in the Persian Gulf?

    a. Kevin Gogan
    b. Jeff Zimmerman
    c. Billy Owens
    d. Chad Hennings

11. Defensive end Tony Tolbert was thrilled to stay close to home when the Cowboys drafted him. Which Texas college did he attend?

    a. Texas Tech
    b. Texas A&M
    c. University of Texas at El Paso
    d. Rice University

12. Running back Calvin Hill was a roommate of future president George W. Bush during his time at Yale.

   a. True
   b. False

13. In 1998 and 1999, the Cowboys spent 1st round draft picks on Greg Ellis and Ebenezer Ekuban; two defensive ends who both came out of which school?

   a. UCLA
   b. Florida State
   c. Duke
   d. North Carolina

14. Two-time Super Bowl champion and Hall of Fame Cowboys quarterback Roger Staubach won the Heisman Trophy while playing where?

   a. Stanford
   b. UCLA
   c. Navy
   d. Wisconsin

15. The Cowboys have drafted more players from which college than anywhere else?

   a. UCLA
   b. Tennessee
   c. Florida
   d. Texas

16. Thomas "Hollywood" Henderson went to school very near Hollywood, at UCLA.

a. True

b. False

17. Which recent Cowboy starter went to college at Mississippi State?

    a. Dak Prescott

    b. Amari Cooper

    c. Byron Jones

    d. Travis Frederick

18. The most players chosen by the Cowboys in a single year from a single college is three, in 2002. Where did these three (Tyson Walter, Jamar Martin, and Derek Ross) go to school?

    a. Florida State

    b. Penn State

    c. Ohio State

    d. Boise State

19. As of 2019, Dallas had selected players from how many different colleges in franchise history?

    a. 96

    b. 138

    c. 170

    d. 217

20. Dallas has selected more players from foreign countries than players from the state of Texas.

    a. True

    b. False

QUIZ ANSWERS

1. C – Miami

2. A – True

3. D – Eastern Illinois

4. C – Yale

5. B – Ed Jones

6. A – Notre Dame

7. B – False

8. A – DB Josh Thomas

9. B – Ohio State University

10. D – Chad Hennings

11. C – University of Texas at El Paso

12. B – False

13. D – North Carolina

14. C – Navy

15. B – Tennessee

16. B – False

17. A – Dak Prescott

18. C – Ohio State

19. D – 217

20. B – False

DID YOU KNOW?

1. Dallas has selected five players in the 1st round who have come from Texas colleges. Bob Lilly played at TCU, Scott Appleton at Texas, Duane Thomas at West Texas State, and Billy Cannon Jr. and Kevin Smith from Texas A&M.

2. Dallas saw something in a Kentucky wide receiver in 1967 and drafted him in the 11th round. Pat Riley would never play football, but he did establish himself as one of the best head coaches and general managers in the NBA, where he holds 6 championship rings.

3. One Dallas native to be selected by the Cowboys was Guy Reese. He was a defensive tackle out of SMU whom the team chose in the 15th round, in 1962.

4. Cowboys linebacker Lee Roy Jordan played for legendary coach Bear Bryant at Alabama. Bryant glowingly said Jordan "was one of the finest football players the world has ever seen. If runners stayed between the sidelines, he tackled them. He never had a bad day."

5. Future Cowboys wide receiver Dez Bryant was suspended for a season in college at Oklahoma State, because he failed to disclose his interactions with former Cowboy Deion Sanders.

6. Dallas coach Jimmy Johnson helped persuade the Cowboys to select six Miami Hurricanes whom he had coached while at the school before leaving for the NFL in

1989. Michael Irvin, Randy Shannon, Rod Carter, Jimmie Jones, Mike Sullivan, and Russell Maryland all joined the coach in both settings.

7. The Cowboys have had players on their roster from both Eastern Illinois (Tony Romo) and Western Illinois (Lance Lenoir Jr.), schools that are not known as traditional football powerhouses.

8. Both Oklahoma State and Wyoming use the nickname "Cowboys," which means that Dallas has selected 10 players whose nickname did not change upon joining the NFL.

9. Five of the first seven Dallas draft choices in history came from schools in Texas. Bob Lilly played at TCU, E.J. Holub at Texas Tech, Sonny Davis at Baylor, Don Talbert at Texas, and Glynn Gregory at SMU.

10. Only five players have ever been drafted to the NFL out of Northwestern Oklahoma State. Dallas chose WR Patrick Crayton from there in 2004, and he lasted seven years in the league.

CHAPTER 11:

IN THE DRAFT ROOM

QUIZ TIME!

1. How many times have the Cowboys held the 1st overall pick in the NFL Draft?

    a. 0

    b. 1

    c. 3

    d. 6

2. The Cowboys have drafted 12 players who made it to the Hall of Fame. No two came from the same school.

    a. True

    b. False

3. When the Cowboys began using computer systems to rank their draft prospects, only one player ever earned a perfect score. Who was it?

    a. Troy Aikman

    b. Deion Sanders

    c. Emmitt Smith

    d. Tony Dorsett

4. In the 2014 NFL Draft, Dallas chose guard Zack Martin 16th overall. Who did owner Jerry Jones famously want to pick instead?

    a. Teddy Bridgewater
    b. Johnny Manziel
    c. C.J. Mosley
    d. Derek Carr

5. In 1988, 1989, and 1990, the Cowboys chose three Hall-of-Famers in the 1st round of the NFL Draft. Which order were they selected in?

    a. Michael Irvin, Troy Aikman, Emmitt Smith
    b. Troy Aikman, Emmitt Smith, Michael Irvin
    c. Emmitt Smith, Michael Irvin, Troy Aikman
    d. Michael Irvin, Emmitt Smith, Troy Aikman

6. The 2015 Dallas draft choice Byron Jones set a world record during his scouting combine testing. What was the record set in?

    a. 40-yard dash
    b. Bench press
    c. Broad jump
    d. Vertical jump

7. Dallas made at least one draft pick trade every year of its existence until 1978, when it kept every single pick.

    a. True
    b. False

8. Hall of Fame wide receiver Bob Hayes was selected in which round of the NFL Draft?

a. 1st round

b. 3rd round

c. 5th round

d. 7th round

9. How many years had the Cowboys gone without selecting a kicker before taking Nick Folk during the 6th round in 2007?

a. 20 years

b. 30 years

c. 40 years

d. 50 years

10. Which player was selected highest in their respective draft class?

a. Tyron Smith

b. Roy Williams

c. Dez Bryant

d. Ezekiel Elliott

11. The Cowboys chose which three offensive linemen in the 1st round within a four-year period?

a. Larry Allen, Mark Stepnoski, and Erik Williams

b. Scott Appleton, John Nilan, and Curtis Marker

c. Robert Shaw, Nate Newton, and Howard Richards

d. Tyron Smith, Travis Frederick, and Zack Martin

12. The first ever draft pick made by the Cowboys became a Pro Football Hall of Fame player.

a. True

b. False

13. Why was franchise quarterback Roger Staubach not drafted until the 10th round of the 1964 draft?

    a. Concerns about his size
    b. Concerns about his medical history
    c. Concerns about his military obligations
    d. Concerns about his likelihood of signing

14. Troy Aikman was selected 1st overall by the Cowboys in which year's entry draft?

    a. 1991
    b. 1989
    c. 1976
    d. 1993

15. Dallas draft pick Pat Toomay wrote a book about his NFL career (including five years with the Cowboys) that became a major Hollywood movie. What was it called?

    a. *On Any Given Sunday*
    b. *The Replacements*
    c. *Leatherheads*
    d. *Invincible*

16. Round 4 is the highest the Cowboys have ever drafted a kicker. He was promptly cut after training camp.

    a. True
    b. False

17. In the 1975 NFL Draft, Dallas took Hall of Fame defensive tackle Randy White 2nd overall. Which team passed on him to draft quarterback Steve Bartkowski instead?

a. Atlanta Falcons

b. Green Bay Packers

c. Philadelphia Eagles

d. San Diego Chargers

18. In the 2017 NFL Draft, the Cowboys selected Vidaunte Charlton, who was better known by what edible nickname?

a. Choco

b. Taco

c. Beansy

d. Milkshake

19. Guard Larry Allen, a contender for best offensive lineman in NFL history, slipped to 46th overall in the draft due to what college injury?

a. Broken leg

b. Turf toe

c. Torn rotator cuff

d. Achilles tendon strain

20. During the 1966 NFL Draft, the Cowboys used 16 of their 19 picks on offensive players, including eight running backs.

a. True

b. False

QUIZ ANSWERS

1. C – 3

2. A – True

3. D – Tony Dorsett

4. B – Johnny Manziel

5. A – Michael Irvin, Troy Aikman, Emmitt Smith

6. C – Broad jump

7. A – True

8. D – 7th round

9. A – 20 years

10. D – Ezekiel Elliott

11. D – Tyron Smith, Travis Frederick, and Zack Martin

12. A – True

13. C – Concerns about his military obligations

14. B – 1989

15. A – *On Any Given Sunday*

16. A – True

17. A – Atlanta Falcons

18. B – Taco

19. C – Torn rotator cuff

20. A – True

DID YOU KNOW?

1. Dallas had such success converting sprinter Bob Hayes into a wide receiver, that in 1984 they used their last draft choice on sprinter Carl Lewis. Like Hayes, Lewis would earn multiple Olympic gold medals. Unlike Hayes, Lewis never did play for the team.

2. Offensive lineman Rayfield Wright was chosen 182nd overall in the NFL Draft, so not much was expected of him. He went on to 6 Pro Bowls, 3 All-Pro selections, the 1970s' All-Decade Team, and the Pro Football Hall of Fame. Not bad for a late pick!

3. The 2018 NFL Draft was the first ever to be held in any stadium. The new home of the Cowboys, AT&T Stadium, set records that night for both televised ratings and in-person attendance.

4. To find receiving help for QB Troy Aikman, Dallas traded its 1st round picks in 2000 and 2001 to Seattle in exchange for wide receiver Joey Galloway. It flopped. Galloway got hurt in his Cowboy debut, and Aikman had retired by the time he came back.

5. The Cowboys have a penchant for choosing defensive linemen high in the draft. Of the franchise's 55 1st round picks, 17 have been either defensive tackles or defensive ends, which is the highest of any position group.

6. In 1990, Dallas selected NFL all-time leading rusher

Emmitt Smith 17th overall. Sixteen teams passed on him, including the New York Jets, who took running back Blair Thomas with their 2nd overall pick instead.

7. The Cowboys passed on WR Randy Moss in the 1998 Draft, after many headaches with similarly troubled WR Michael Irvin. Moss went 7-0 in his career against Dallas, with 10 touchdowns scored.

8. In their first five drafts, the Cowboys selected seven men named Jim, along with seven named Bob. The tie was broken the following year when Bob Dunlevy was selected. There would not be another Jim for several years.

9. Ninth round draft choice Kenneth Gant carved out an 8-year NFL career and was a Cowboys standout on special teams. Known as "The Shark," Gant would break out his "Shark Dance" after big plays to fire up the crowd.

10. Colston Weatherington owns the longest name ever pronounced at the podium by Dallas on draft day. He and his 20 letters were selected during round 7 of the 2001 Draft.

CHAPTER 12:

THE TRADING POST

QUIZ TIME!

1. Dallas traded a 3rd round pick in the 1990 Draft in order to move up how many spots in the 1st round to select franchise legend Emmitt Smith?

    a. 2
    b. 4
    c. 7
    d. 13

2. For four consecutive years in the 1970s, the Cowboys traded out of the 1st round of the NFL Draft, acquiring more proven talent in an effort to compete with the Pittsburgh Steelers.

    a. True
    b. False

3. Which Dallas quarterback was moved to the New York Giants to make way for Roger Staubach after Staubach had fulfilled his military obligations?

a. Eddie LeBaron
b. Danny White
c. Troy Aikman
d. Craig Morton

4. Which WR did Dallas acquire from Tampa Bay in a straight-up trade for WR Joey Galloway?

a. Keyshawn Johnson
b. Michael Clayton
c. Tim Brown
d. Alvin Harper

5. Which key piece of Dallas's Super Bowl winning team did not come from one of the draft picks acquired in the famous Herschel Walker deal with Minnesota?

a. Emmitt Smith
b. Russell Maryland
c. Larry Brown
d. Darren Woodson

6. From which franchise did Dallas acquire QB Jon Kitna as a backup for Tony Romo in 2009?

a. Cincinnati Bengals
b. Seattle Seahawks
c. New Orleans Saints
d. Detroit Lions

7. In their entire history, the Cowboys have never traded away a player who was born in the state of Texas.

a. True
b. False

8. Which team did the Cowboys trade up with so they could select RB Tony Dorsett at the NFL Draft?

   a. New Orleans Saints
   b. Denver Broncos
   c. Pittsburgh Steelers
   d. Seattle Seahawks

9. Which team did the Cowboys trade up with so they could select RB Emmitt Smith at the NFL Draft?

   a. New Orleans Saints
   b. Denver Broncos
   c. Pittsburgh Steelers
   d. Seattle Seahawks

10. Which wide receiver, currently still with the Cowboys, did the team acquire from the Los Angeles Rams in 2018?

    a. Tavon Austin
    b. Amari Cooper
    c. Michael Gallup
    d. Cedrick Wilson

11. In 2015, the Cowboys made a trade with Seattle to acquire which Texas born and educated running back?

    a. Shaun Alexander
    b. Christine Michael
    c. Julius Jones
    d. DeAndre Washington

12. Dallas has completed more trades involving quarterbacks than any other position.

a. True

b. False

13. In 2008, Dallas traded three draft picks to Detroit for wide receiver Roy Williams. What rounds were those draft choices in?

    a. 1st, 2nd, 4th
    b. 2nd, 2nd, 3rd
    c. 1st, 3rd, 6th
    d. 2nd, 4th, 7th

14. How many draft choices did the Cowboys give up in order to move up and select RB Tony Dorsett?

    a. 1
    b. 2
    c. 3
    d. 4

15. What did Dallas trade to the Oakland Raiders to acquire wide receiver Amari Cooper, who became a franchise cornerstone?

    a. WR Dez Bryant
    b. A 1st round draft choice
    c. A 7th round draft choice and salary cap relief
    d. Future considerations

16. The Cowboys received 8 draft picks when they traded RB Herschel Walker to the Minnesota Vikings in 1989.

    a. True
    b. False

17. Which coach was fired after the Cowboys traded two 1st round picks for receiver Joey Galloway, only to see him tear an ACL in his first game with Dallas?

    a. Wade Phillips

    b. Jimmy Johnson

    c. Dave Campo

    d. Tom Landry

18. After Dallas traded with St. Louis to acquire offensive lineman Alex Barron, they cut him after his very first game with the team. Why?

    a. He tore his MCL and ACL when a defensive lineman fell awkwardly on his leg.

    b. He was late to the game and did not appear until after halftime.

    c. He swore at the referee and was ejected from the contest early in the second quarter.

    d. He committed a holding penalty that negated a game-winning touchdown.

19. In 2015, Dallas turned to Buffalo for some quarterback depth and picked up which backup QB from the Bills?

    a. E.J. Manuel

    b. Matt Cassel

    c. Trent Edwards

    d. J.P. Losman

20. In the span of four days prior to the 2013 NFL season, the Cowboys acquired seven 7th round draft picks from the

Chiefs, Chargers, and Bears, then shipped one of them to the Indianapolis Colts.

a. True
b. False

QUIZ ANSWERS

1. B – 4

2. B – False

3. D – Craig Morton

4. A – Keyshawn Johnson

5. C – Larry Brown

6. D – Detroit Lions

7. B – False

8. D – Seattle Seahawks

9. C – Pittsburgh Steelers

10. A – Tavon Austin

11. B – Christine Michael

12. B – False

13. C – 1st, 3rd, 6th

14. D – 4

15. B – A 1st round draft choice

16. A – True

17. C – Dave Campo

18. D – He committed a holding penalty that negated a game-winning touchdown.

19. B – Matt Cassel

20. A – False

DID YOU KNOW?

1. While the Cowboys were winning in the 1970s, they pulled off two trades with the much worse Houston Oilers and New York Giants. In exchange for small pieces, they acquired 1st round picks from each team, which turned out to be 1st overall and 2nd overall. Dallas got two strong defensive linemen with those picks, Too Tall Jones and Randy White, who combined for 12 All-Pro selections.

2. In 1989, head coach Jimmy Johnson orchestrated the biggest player trade in the history of the NFL when he sent stud running back Herschel Walker to the Minnesota Vikings in exchange for several players and draft picks. Many Cowboys fans were skeptical of the decision to ship off such an elite talent as Walker, but the pieces acquired by Dallas, including Emmitt Smith, were key to their three championships won in the '90s.

3. This Herschel Walker trade was so significant, ESPN made a documentary film about it as part of its acclaimed *30 for 30* series. The movie was called *The Great Trade Robbery*.

4. Dallas fans were salivating over two-sport star Drew Henson (who was also drafted by baseball's New York Yankees). Many were thrilled when the team made a trade with the Houston Texans to acquire his rights.

Unfortunately, Henson started only one game at QB for the Cowboys before moving on to NFL Europe.

5. The Cowboys probably made a mistake using the 1st pick in the 1989 supplemental draft on QB Steve Walsh. But they recovered nicely by trading Walsh to Tampa Bay for 1st, 2nd, and 3rd round picks. They got good value and used the picks well, but even more importantly, they cleared the way for young QB Troy Aikman to play and lead the team to three Super Bowls.

6. Star offensive tackle Ralph Neely was originally drafted by the Baltimore Colts. The Colts traded his rights to Dallas for two-way player Billy Lothridge and a 4th round pick because they feared he might sign with the AFL's Houston Oilers instead.

7. Over the span of a few months in 2018, the Cowboys sent out one Ward and brought in another. CB Charvarius Ward was traded to Kansas City, while DT Jihad Ward was acquired from Oakland.

8. Jimmy Johnson nearly traded franchise icon Michael Irvin to the Oakland Raiders, but reconsidered when Oakland owner Al Davis asked him, "You sure you want to do that? He can smell the end zone."

9. Dallas traded up with St. Louis for the valuable 6th overall pick in the 2012 NFL Draft and used it to take cornerback Morris Claiborne, who never played a full season or recorded more than one interception per year for the team. The Rams used the Cowboys' pick on DE Michael Brockers, who remains with the team today.

10. The Dallas Cowboys knew they were getting a major steal when they shipped RB Herschel Walker to the Minnesota Vikings. But Walker did not want to go. The Cowboys paid him a $1.25 million exit bonus to convince him to agree to the trade.

CHAPTER 13:

SUPER BOWL SPECIAL

QUIZ TIME!

1. Who was the Cowboys' first ever Super Bowl MVP?

   a. Tony Dorsett

   b. Chuck Howley

   c. Roger Staubach

   d. Randy White

2. Dallas is the first NFL team to win the Super Bowl after losing the previous year.

   a. True

   b. False

3. Which Cowboys quarterback is 3-0 in Super Bowls, better than any NFL QB except Terry Bradshaw?

   a. Roger Staubach

   b. Don Meredith

   c. Craig Morton

   d. Troy Aikman

4. Which team has defeated the Cowboys twice in the Super Bowl?

    a. Pittsburgh Steelers
    b. New England Patriots
    c. Buffalo Bills
    d. Miami Dolphins

5. The Cowboys have played three Super Bowls in this venue and lost all three.

    a. Superdome, New Orleans
    b. Colosseum, Los Angeles
    c. Orange Bowl, Miami
    d. Rose Bowl, Pasadena

6. What is the average margin of victory that the Cowboys have posted in their five Super Bowl wins?

    a. 2 points
    b. 9 points
    c. 13 points
    d. 20 points

7. Dallas is the first team to lose the Super Bowl after winning it the previous year.

    a. True
    b. False

8. What is the most points the Cowboys have scored in any Super Bowl?

    a. 32 points
    b. 42 points

    c. 52 points

    d. 62 points

9. Dallas has played in the Super Bowl eight times, which is more than every other NFL franchise except which?

    a. Pittsburgh Steelers

    b. New England Patriots

    c. Denver Broncos

    d. Minnesota Vikings

10. Which opponent did the Cowboys defeat in two consecutive Super Bowls?

    a. Kansas City Chiefs

    b. Miami Dolphins

    c. Denver Broncos

    d. Buffalo Bills

11. Against the Miami Dolphins, Bob Lilly sacked QB Bob Griese well behind the line of scrimmage for what is still the longest negative play in Super Bowl history. How far back did Lilly take him down?

    a. 18 yards

    b. 23 yards

    c. 29 yards

    d. 37 yards

12. The Cowboys have appeared in more Super Bowls than the three other teams in the NFC East combined.

    a. True

    b. False

13. During their three Super Bowl defeats, what is the average margin the Cowboys have lost by?

    a. 1 point
    b. 4 points
    c. 17 points
    d. 25 points

14. Of the five Cowboys Super Bowl Championships, which was won by the largest margin?

    a. Super Bowl XXVII
    b. Super Bowl XXX
    c. Super Bowl VI
    d. Super Bowl XII

15. Dallas has won Super Bowls in each of these states except for which one?

    a. Arizona
    b. Texas
    c. Louisiana
    d. Georgia

16. The Cowboys are undefeated in Super Bowl games held in a dome.

    a. True
    b. False

17. During Super Bowl XIII, this rookie cornerback recovered a key onside kick against the Steelers.

    a. Terence Newman
    b. Everson Walls

c. Dennis Thurman

d. Ron Fellows

18. Which of the following players has NOT won a Super Bowl MVP with the Cowboys?

    a. Troy Aikman

    b. Emmitt Smith

    c. Tony Dorsett

    d. Roger Staubach

19. Before Bart Starr passed away in 2019, this Cowboy was the only Super Bowl MVP to have died.

    a. Chuck Howley

    b. Harvey Martin

    c. Larry Brown

    d. Roger Staubach

20. The Dallas Cowboys have appeared in twice as many Super Bowls as the Buffalo Bills, but have still allowed fewer total points in the Super Bowl.

    a. True

    b. False

QUIZ ANSWERS

1. B – Chuck Howley

2. A – True

3. D – Troy Aikman

4. A – Pittsburgh Steelers

5. C – Orange Bowl, Miami

6. D – 20 points

7. A – True

8. C – 52 points

9. B – New England Patriots

10. D – Buffalo Bills

11. C – 29 yards

12. B – False

13. B – 4 points

14. A – Super Bowl XXVII

15. B – Texas

16. A – True

17. C – Dennis Thurman

18. C – Tony Dorsett

19. B – Harvey Martin

20. A – True

DID YOU KNOW?

1. After a Super Bowl loss to the Baltimore Colts, Cowboys defensive end Bob Lilly lost his cool and tossed his helmet 40 yards across the field. He felt quite embarrassed afterward, especially when a Colts rookie handed it back, saying, "Here's your helmet, Mr. Lilly."

2. The Cowboys have the highest positive points differential in the Super Bowl among any NFL franchise, at +89. Only the arch-rival San Francisco 49ers are anywhere close, at +85.

3. Leon Lett's most famous moment occurred during the Super Bowl in 1993. Lett recovered a fumble and rumbled down the field for an easy touchdown. But he slowed down early to celebrate, and a hustling Don Beebe ran him down to strip the ball. Lett later filmed a Snickers commercial poking fun at the moment.

4. In 1972, Dallas defeated the Miami Dolphins in Super Bowl VI, 24-3, becoming the first team to hold its opponent without a touchdown in the championship game.

5. The legendary Emmitt Smith holds the record for most career rushing touchdowns in the Super Bowl. In three games, he scored five times.

6. Chuck Howley is the only player in NFL history to have won the Super Bowl MVP while playing on the losing team. Howley had two interceptions in Super Bowl V,

which the Cowboys eventually lost 16-13 to the Baltimore Colts.

7. Howley is also the first non-quarterback in NFL history to be named Super Bowl MVP.

8. QB Troy Aikman has the NFL's all-time highest completion percentage in Super Bowls, converting 70% of his passes.

9. In eight Super Bowl appearances, only two opposing players have won the MVP award against Dallas. Both of them came from the Pittsburgh Steelers dynasty of the 1970s; Lynn Swann and Terry Bradshaw.

10. During Super Bowl XXVII, Dallas scored a whopping seven touchdowns against the Buffalo Bills. Placekicker Lin Elliott etched his name in the record books by converting all seven extra point attempts.

CHAPTER 14:

THE FINAL WORDS

QUIZ TIME!

1. Some of coach Tom Landry's best advice was expressed when he explained: "When you want to win a game, you have to teach. When you lose a game, you have to _____."

   a. Teach a bit more

   b. Go back to school

   c. Feel it

   d. Learn

2. Physical specimen Herschel Walker once described the effort he put into staying in shape as the Cowboys' lead running back thusly: "If you train hard, you'll not only be hard, you'll be hard to beat."

   a. True

   b. False

3. Which Dallas Cowboy popularized the phrase "If ifs and buts were candy and nuts, we'd all have a Merry Christmas" in response to a question about the NFL playoff standings?

a. Cliff Harris

b. Don Meredith

c. Too Tall Jones

d. Bob Hayes

4. Which wide receiver said, upon joining the Cowboys, "I'm a star among stars now. Hey, just get your popcorn ready because it's going to be a show!"?

   a. Dez Bryant

   b. Drew Pearson

   c. Terrell Owens

   d. Cole Beasley

5. Which Dallas Cowboys leader once said, "Leadership is getting someone to do what they don't want to do, to achieve what they want to achieve."?

   a. Roger Staubach

   b. Tom Landry

   c. Jimmy Johnson

   d. Troy Aikman

6. Many people thought that this Cowboys coach could have been referring to himself inheriting a talented roster when he said, "Some people are born on third base and go through life thinking they hit a triple."

   a. Barry Switzer

   b. Dave Campo

   c. Jason Garrett

   d. Wade Phillips

7. Tough tight end Mike Ditka once remarked about a lack of effort being shown by saying, "If things came easy, then everybody would be great at what they did, let's face it."

   a. True
   b. False

8. Which of the following is NOT a quote from quarterback Roger Staubach about the importance of hard work?

   a. "I was 0-11 as a rookie starter, but we didn't throw in the towel. We all pulled together to do whatever was necessary to succeed."
   b. "There are no traffic jams along the extra mile."
   c. "In any team sport, the best teams have consistency and chemistry."
   d. "Winning isn't getting ahead of others. It's getting ahead of yourself."

9. Cowboys executive Gil Brandt put his own spin on a popular song by saying, "Mommas, let your babies grow up to be ____."

   a. Cowboys
   b. Cowboys fans
   c. Left tackles
   d. Anything but Redskins

10. Quarterback Don Meredith once comically remarked about his running back's consistency: "If you needed 4 yards, you'd give the ball to him and he would get you 4 yards. If you needed 20 yards, you'd give the ball to him

and he would get you 4 yards." Which running back was he referring to?

   a. Tony Dorsett

   b. Calvin Hill

   c. Walt Garrison

   d. Don Perkins

11. Coach Jimmy Johnson always wanted to win. He reminded his players with the saying: "The difference between ordinary and extraordinary is _____."

   a. Putting in the work

   b. That little extra

   c. Fighting till the clock runs out

   d. Remembering you're a Dallas Cowboy

12. WR Michael Irvin often repeated the mantra: "Look up, get up, and don't ever give up."

   a. True

   b. False

13. About which rival quarterback did Hollywood Henderson say, "_____ couldn't spell cat if you spotted him the 'c' and the 't.'"?

   a. Daryl Lamonica

   b. Phil Simms

   c. Fran Tarkenton

   d. Terry Bradshaw

14. What did owner Jerry Jones say upon firing Cowboys head coach Jimmy Johnson in 1994 that created a major rift between the long-time friends?

a. "He's losing his edge…he's gone from one of those Ginsus to a rusty pocket knife."

b. "We'll just see what our record is when his replacement settles into his office."

c. "There are 500 coaches who could have won the Super Bowl with our team."

d. "Jimmy always thought it was all about Jimmy."

15. Which Cowboys coach reminded his players of his philosophy in a speech: "It takes absolutely no talent to hustle or compete. Set that standard."?

a. Tom Landry

b. Jimmy Johnson

c. Wade Phillips

d. Jason Garrett

16. Jenna Bush, daughter of President George W. Bush, revealed her fandom in one interview, stating, "My first cat was named Cowboy, after the Dallas Cowboys."

a. True

b. False

17. Which Cowboy once gloated about the team by saying, "We're the glitz and glamour of the NFL. We want to kick their you know what with glitz and glamour!"?

a. Cornerback Deion Sanders

b. Wide Receiver Dez Bryant

c. Owner Jerry Jones

d. Linebacker Hollywood Henderson

18. Which viciously confident Cowboys wide receiver once said, "I can attack a man's weakness and beat him. Or I can attack a man's strengths and break him."

    a. Michael Irvin
    b. Terrell Owens
    c. Dez Bryant
    d. Bob Hayes

19. What was owner Jerry Jones's comment on finishing 4-12, last in the NFC East, in 2015?

    a. "It's like holding two handfuls of Jell-O and trying to keep it all in those two hands."
    b. "I'm lookin' up, on my back, and all I see is ass. I want a different perspective."
    c. "Whether it's the oil business or the football business, the one place you don't wanna be is at the bottom of a deep, dry hole."
    d. "The Redskins got lucky, the Giants aren't even the best team in their city, and the Eagles can talk to me when they've won five Super Bowls."

20. Cowboys quarterback Troy Aikman expressed his gunslinger's philosophy by saying, "I've never been a fan of this 'manage the game' stuff. It doesn't make sense to pay guys to make plays, then tell them to go out and not make mistakes."

    a. True
    b. False

QUIZ ANSWERS

1. D – Learn

2. A – True

3. B – Don Meredith

4. C – Terrell Owens

5. B – Tom Landry

6. A – Barry Switzer

7. A – True

8. A – "I was 0-11 as a rookie starter, but we didn't throw in the towel. We all pulled together to do whatever was necessary to succeed."

9. C – Left tackles

10. C – Walt Garrison

11. B – That little extra

12. A – True

13. D – Terry Bradshaw

14. C – "There are 500 coaches who could have won the Super Bowl with our team."

15. D – Jason Garrett

16. A – True

17. C – Owner Jerry Jones

18. A – Michael Irvin

19. B – "I'm lookin' up, on my back, and all I see is ass. I want a different perspective."

20. A – True

DID YOU KNOW?

1. Explaining the history of success enjoyed by the Cowboys, general manager Tex Schramm thought it started with the scouting. "We would bring in more free agents than half a dozen other teams combined, and we were very active in scouting the smaller schools. No other team was putting that effort into those schools, and it paid off again and again for us."

2. Franchise icon Roger Staubach was consistently focused on preparation, mentioning that "spectacular achievements come from unspectacular preparation," and that "confidence doesn't come out of nowhere. It's a result of hours and days and weeks and years of constant work and dedication."

3. Commentator Don Meredith once remarked about his former coach's exacted standards: "Tom Landry is such a perfectionist, if he was married to Raquel Welch, he'd expect her to cook."

4. Cornerback Deion Sanders was remarkably fast and effective. Opposing player Ray Horton once said of him, "I think Deion really did revolutionize the man-to-man football game of taking half the field away. What he did in essence was, if you threw the ball his way, he would outrun the ball."

5. Cowboys coach Bill Parcells did not agree with his

predecessor Tom Landry when it came to the value of finding lessons from big losses. Instead, Parcells "never bought into the idea that you learn much from losing. In my experience, you learn far more from winning, which also makes your players more receptive to criticism."

6. Asked if the Cowboys had passed on exciting quarterback Johnny Manziel in the NFL Draft because it might sour current QB Tony Romo's feelings for the team, owner Jerry Jones went off on an epic rant: "What is amazing, if there's anybody on this planet that could have handled Manziel competin' with him...this guy could handle any damn thing! This is your fighter pilot! This is the guy you want goin' in, droppin' and winkin' at 'em, and comin' out, and drinkin' beer. This is him. So he could handle it. It wasn't a question of not handlin' it."

7. When Ezekiel Elliot was chosen high in the NFL Draft, he paid homage to the history of his new franchise and won over fans right away, saying, "I understand what's expected of me. I understand the lineage for the running back position for the Dallas Cowboys."

8. In 2015, owner Jerry Jones was asked how it felt to lose star receiver Dez Bryant to injury in week one, and star quarterback Tony Romo in week two. He responded, "Just about as low as a crippled cricket's ass."

9. During the ongoing feud between Cowboys owner Jerry Jones and former coach Jimmy Johnson, Jones gloated over the success of his new head coach Barry Switzer,

saying, "I'd rather have won that one with Barry 1,000 times more than having done the same thing with Jimmy."

10. Sportswriter Bob Ryan sums up the Cowboys thusly: "They are the Notre Dame of professional football. No matter where they play, their fans are there to greet them. Their faces are recognized by fans all across this country. The sum total of their stars are a galaxy. They are the Dallas Cowboys...America's Team."

CONCLUSION

There you have it; an amazing collection of Cowboys trivia, information, and statistics at your fingertips! Regardless of how you fared on the quizzes, we hope that you found this book entertaining, enlightening, and educational.

Ideally, you knew many of these details, but also learned a good deal more about the history of the Dallas Cowboys, their players, coaches, management, and some of the quirky stories surrounding the team. If you got a little peek into the colorful details that make being a fan so much more enjoyable, then mission accomplished!

The good news is the trivia doesn't have to stop there! Spread the word. Challenge your fellow Cowboys fans to see if they can do any better. Share some of the stories with the next generation to help them become Dallas supporters too.

If you are a big enough Cowboys fan, consider creating your own quiz with some of the details you know that weren't presented here, and then test your friends to see if they can match your knowledge.

The Dallas Cowboys are a storied franchise. They have a long history with many periods of success, and a few that were less than successful. They've had glorious superstars, iconic moments, hilarious tales...but most of all, they have wonderful, passionate fans. Thank you for being one of them.

Made in the USA
Coppell, TX
20 December 2020

46781035R00079